**ISBN-13:
978-1517068059
ISBN-10:
1517068053**

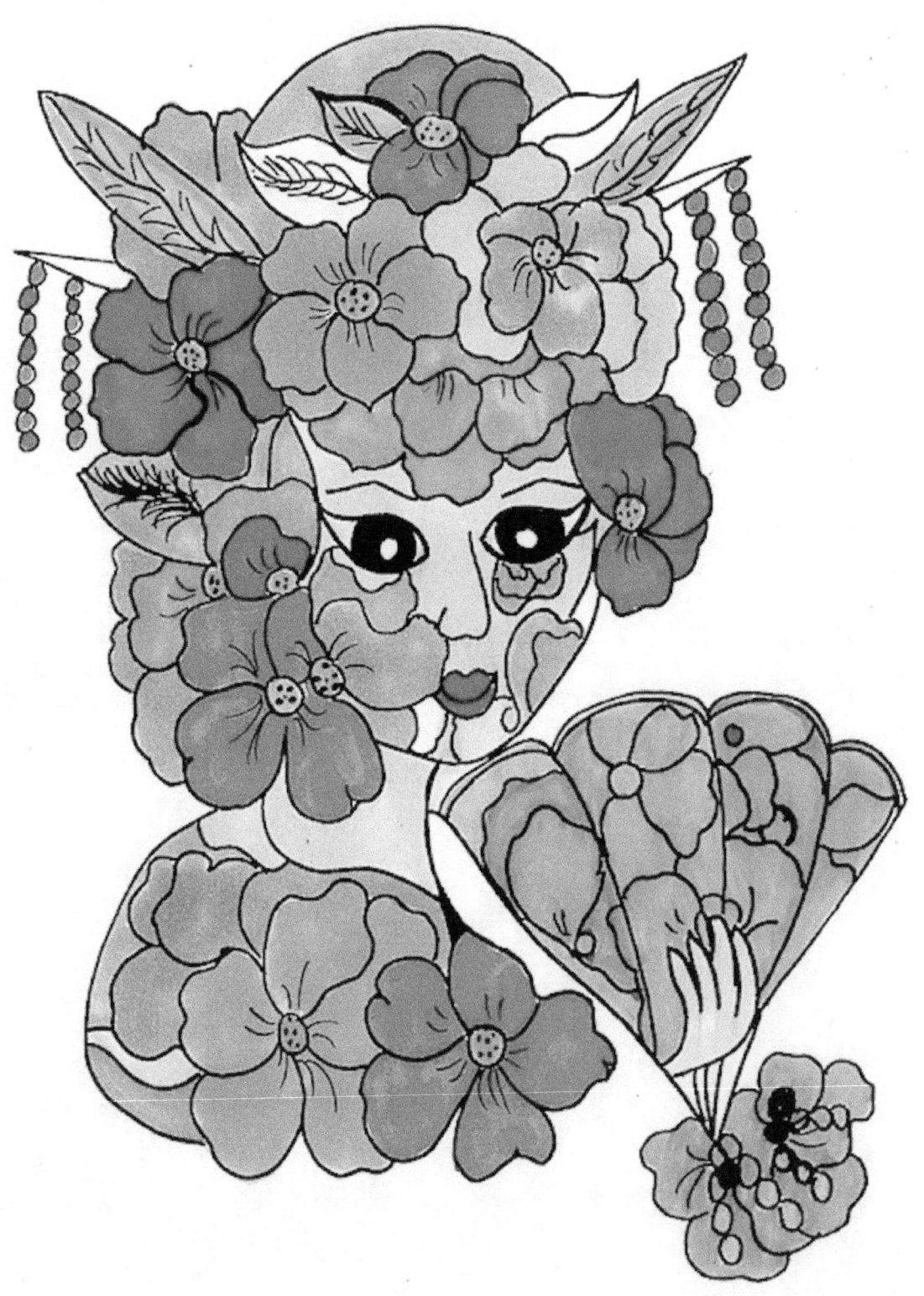

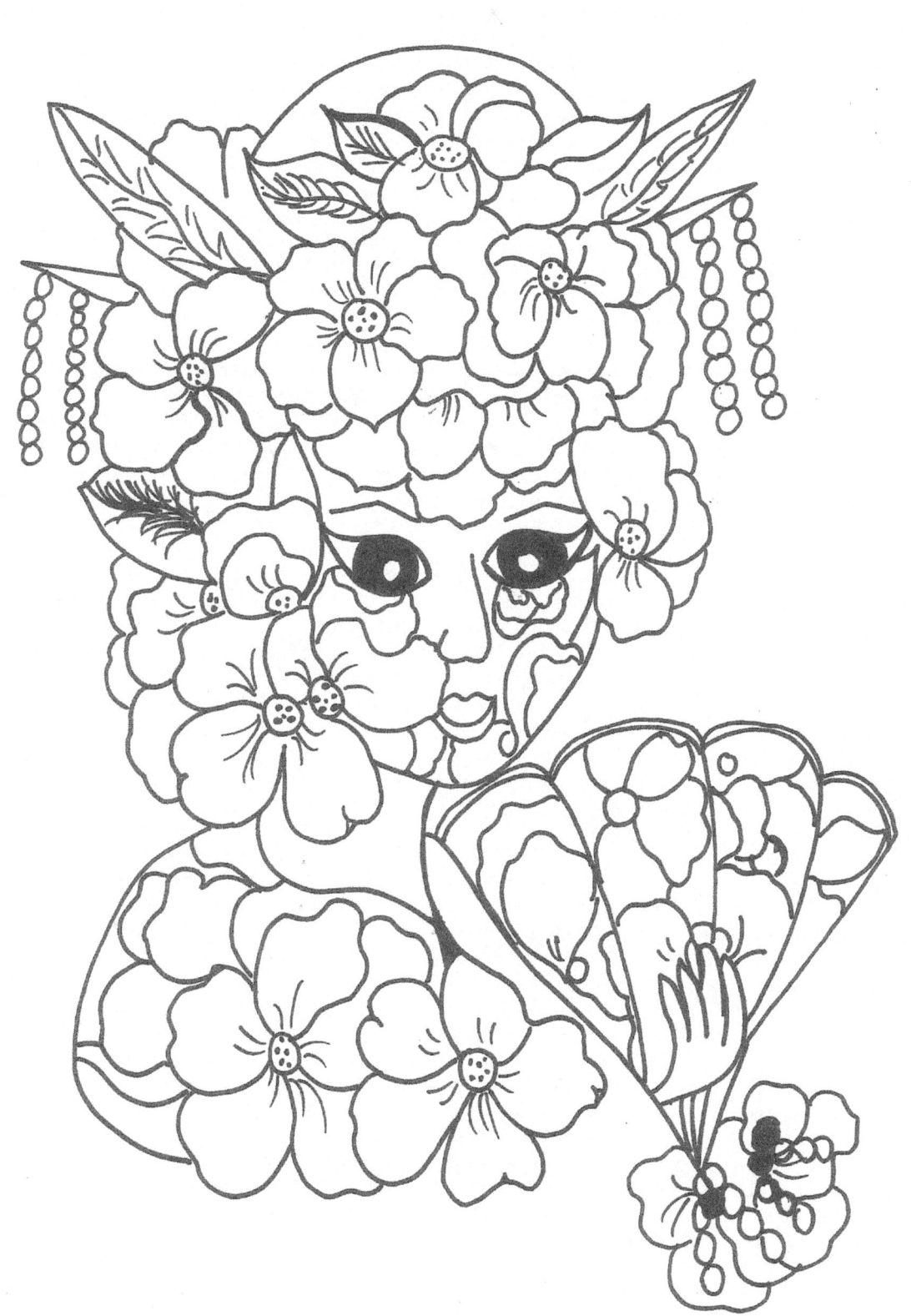

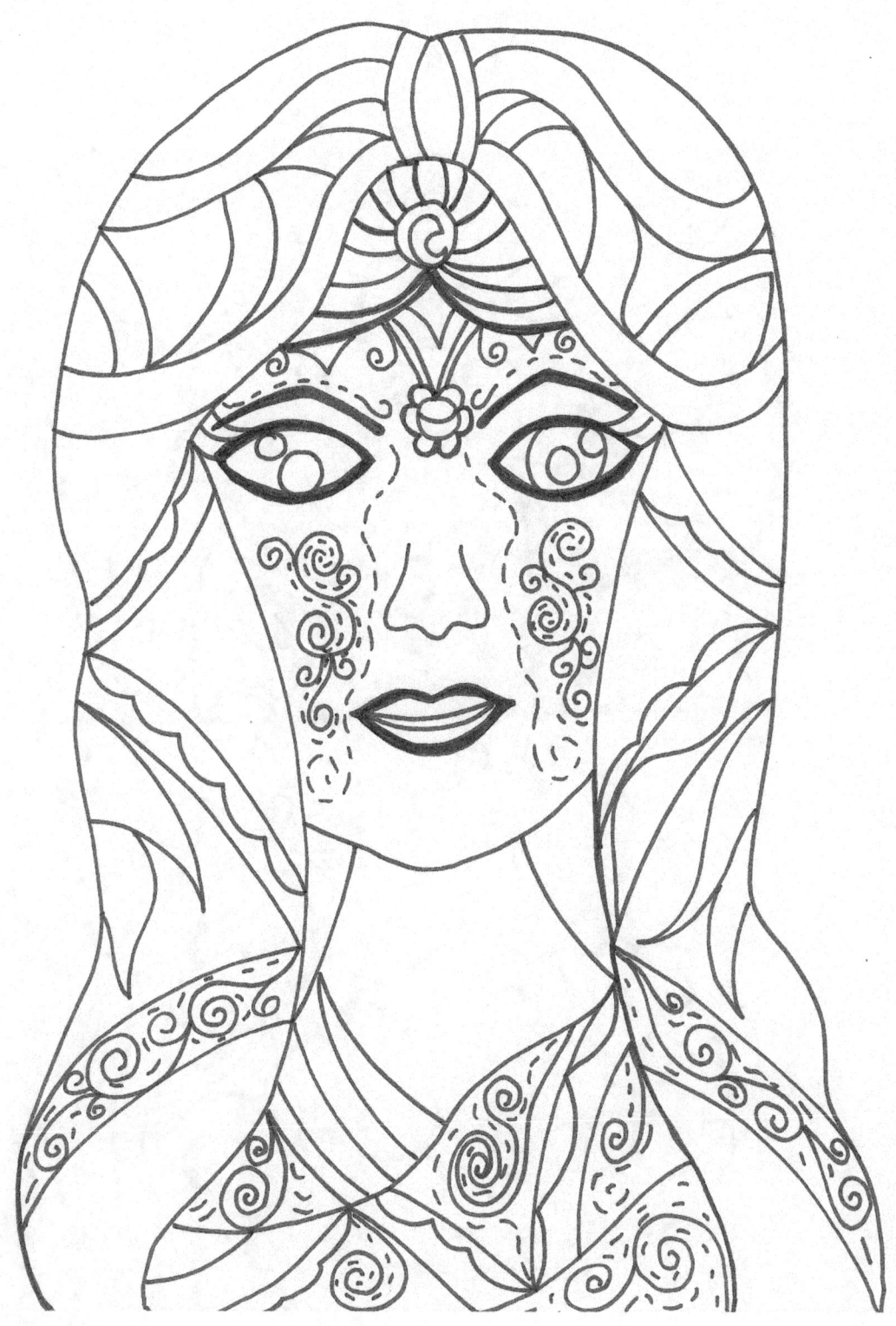

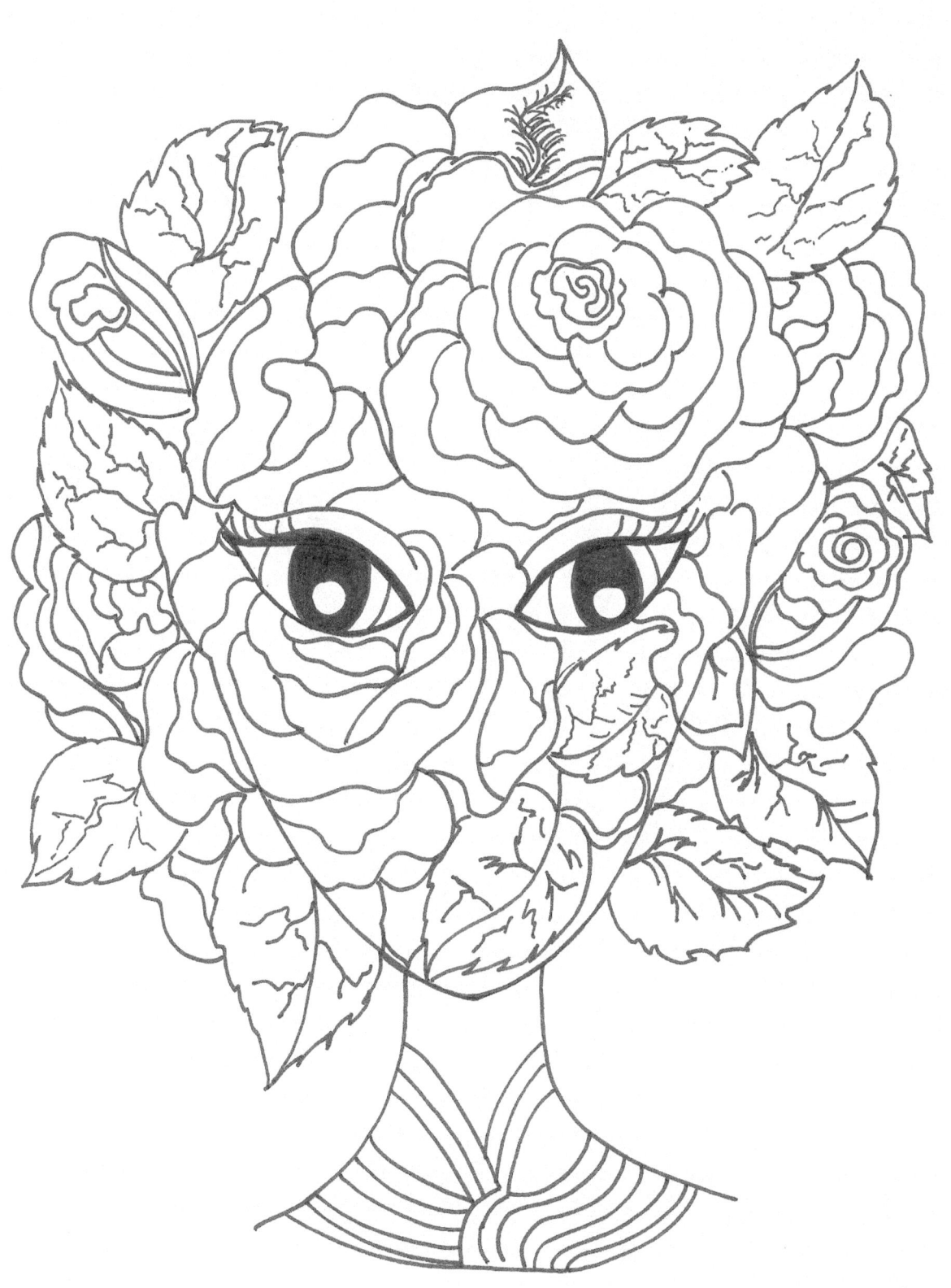

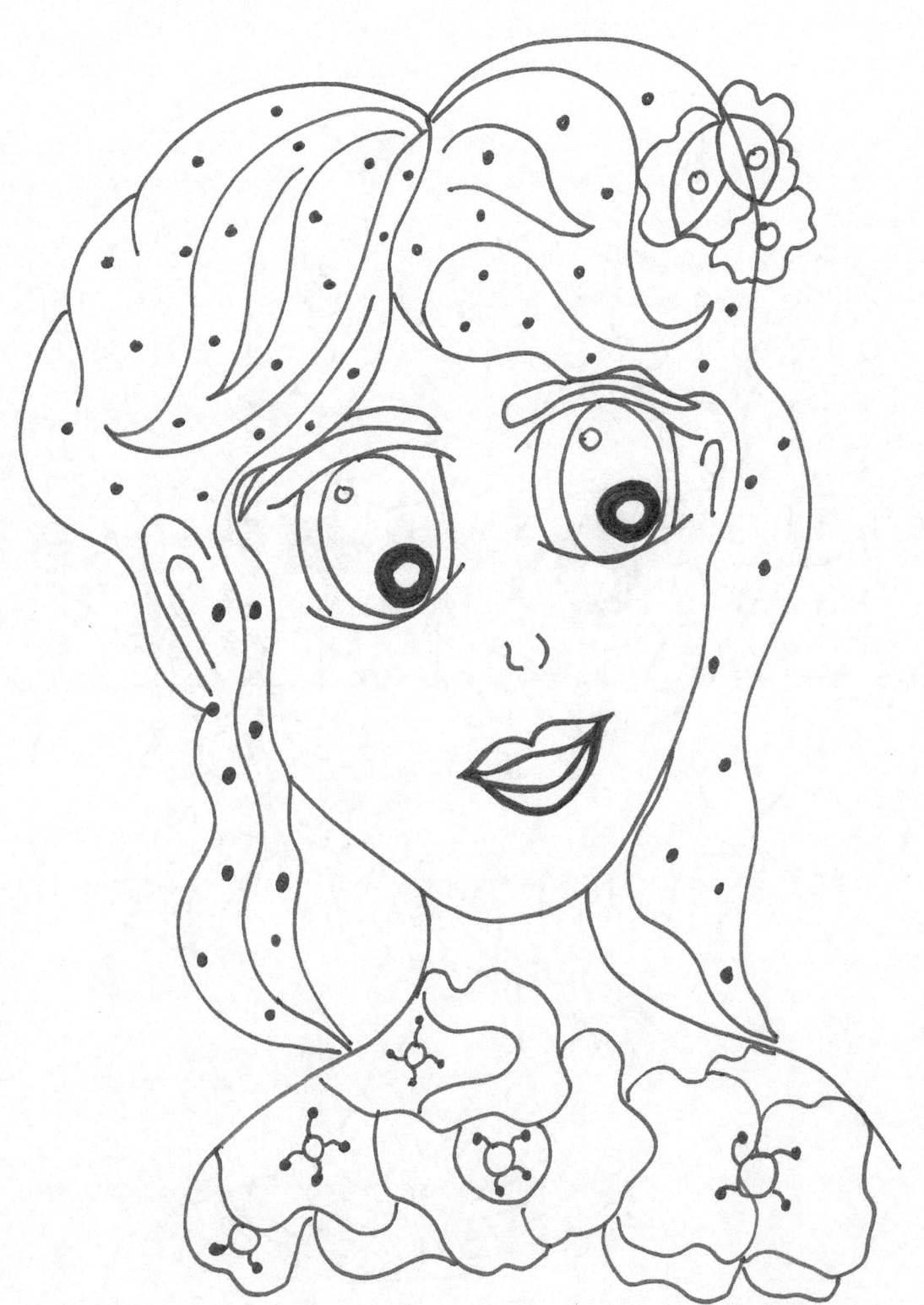

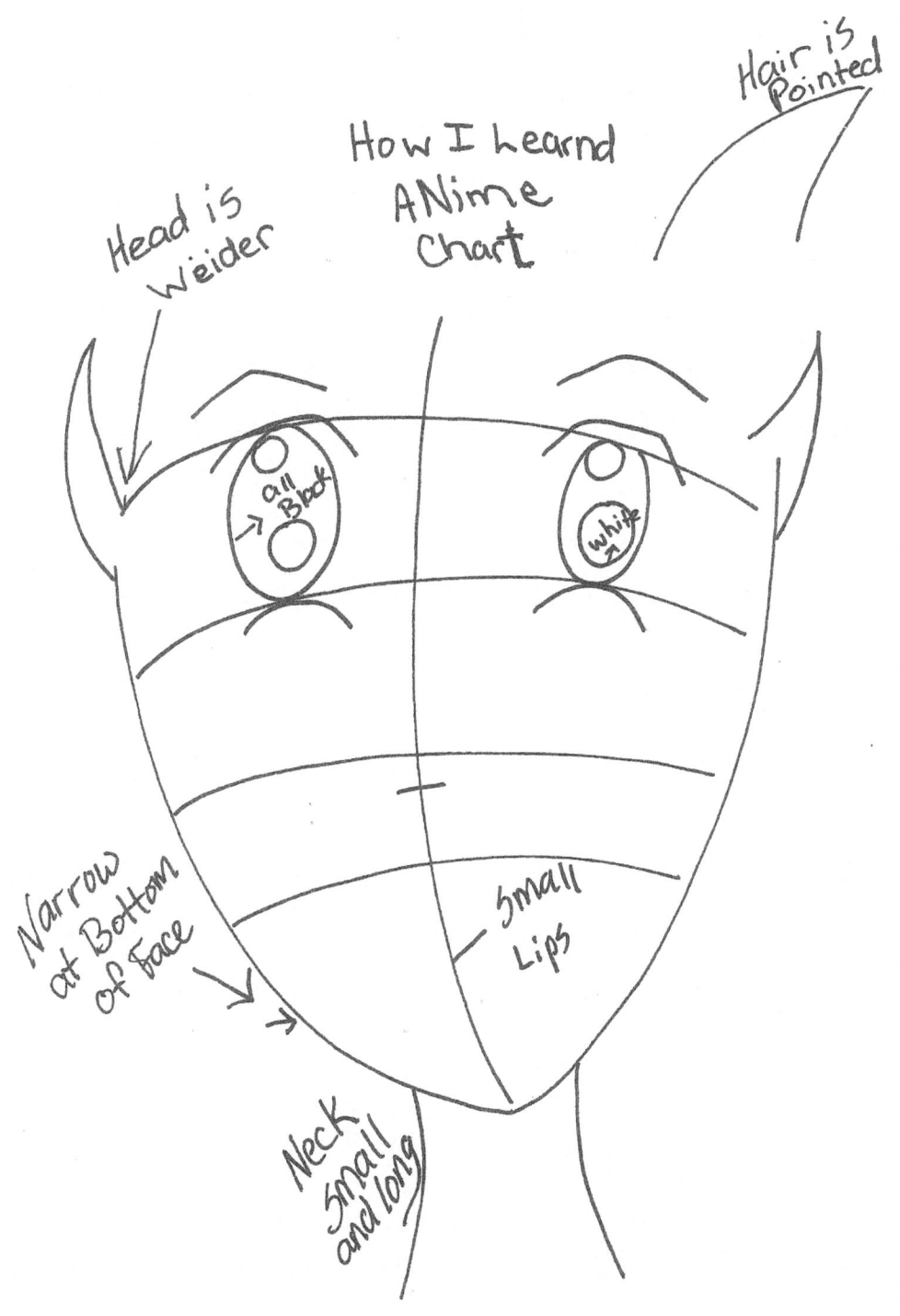

How I Learnd
ANime
Chart

Hair is
Pointed

Head is
Weider

all
Black

white

Narrow
at Bottom
of face

Small
Lips

Neck
Small
and long

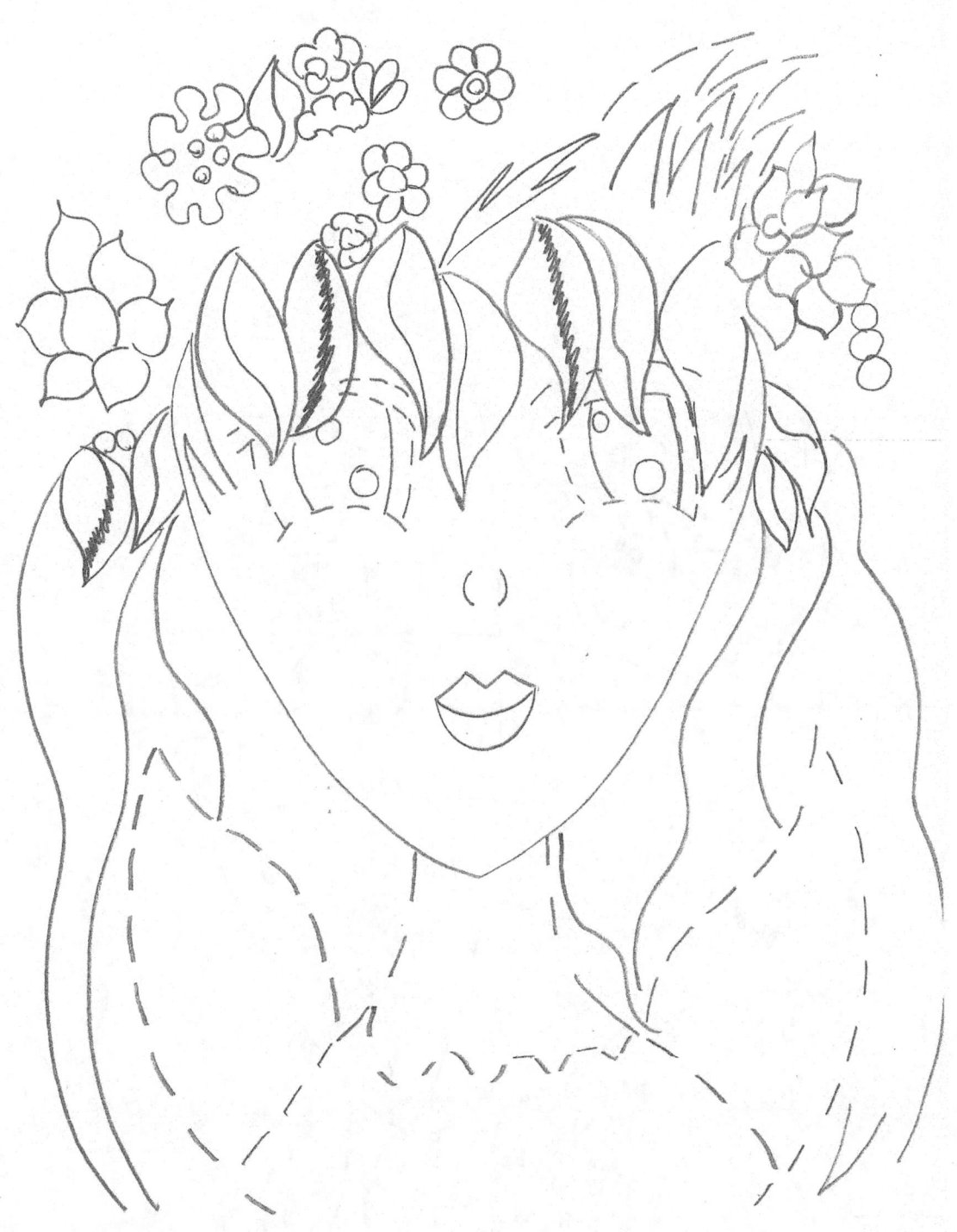

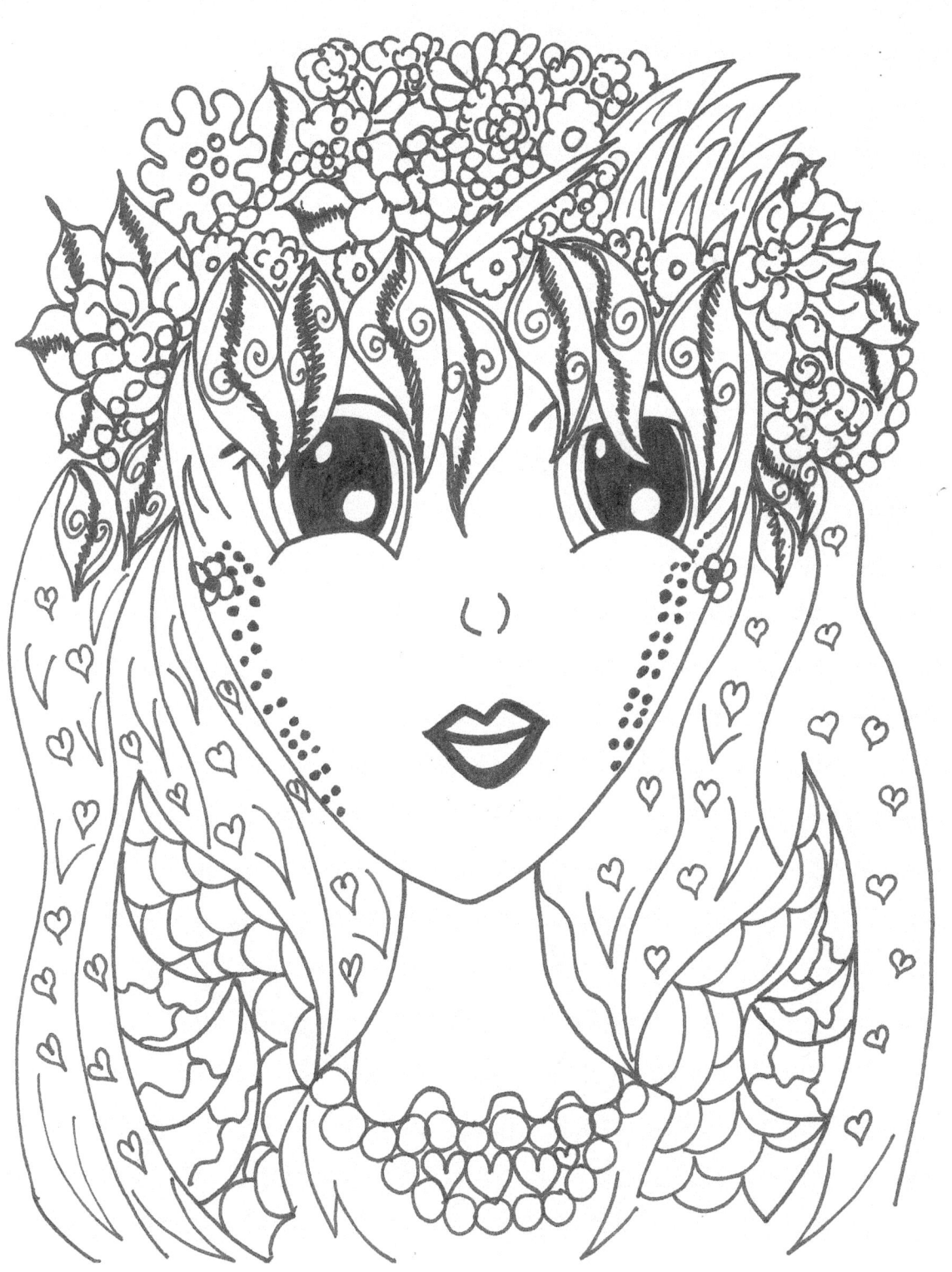

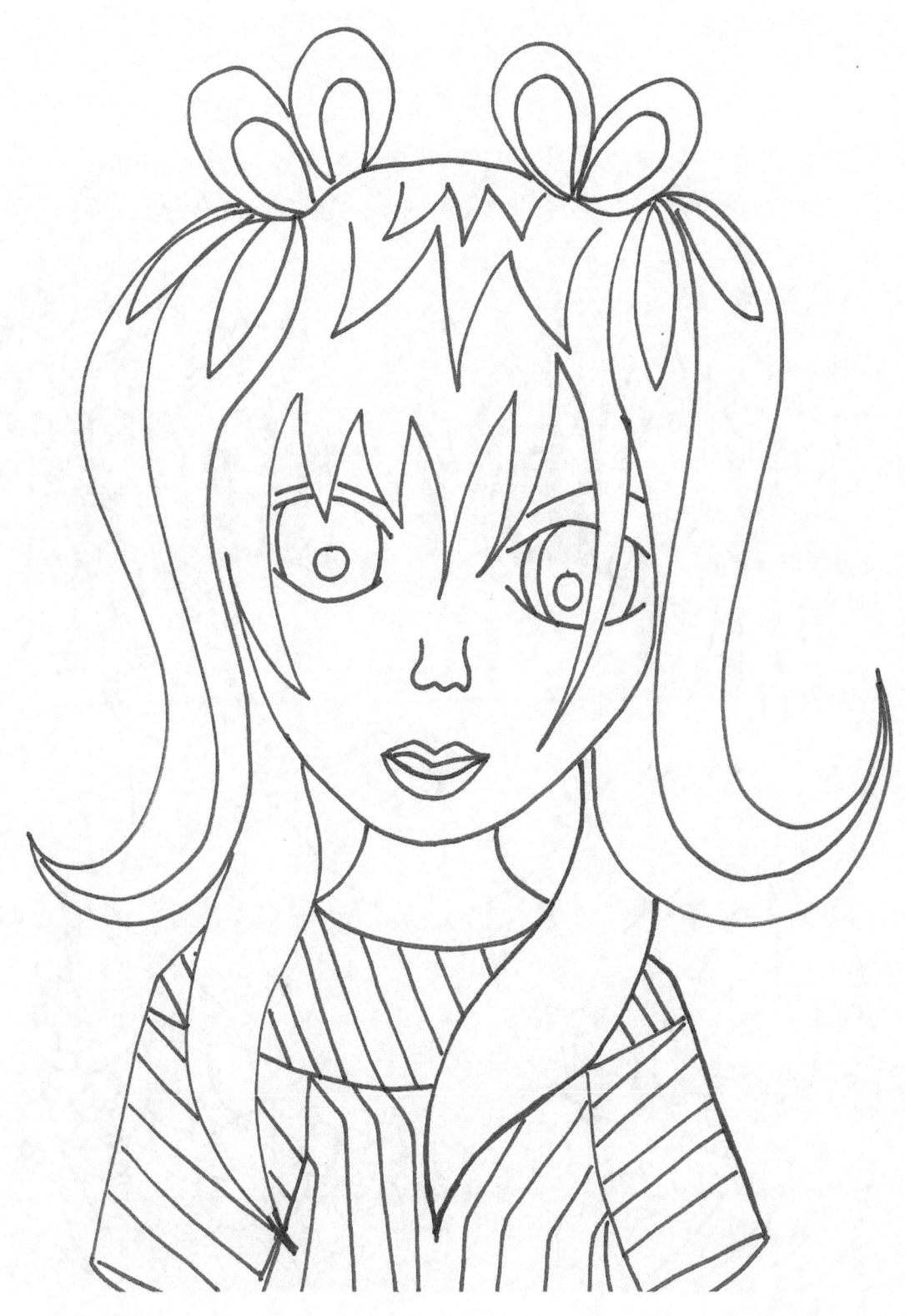

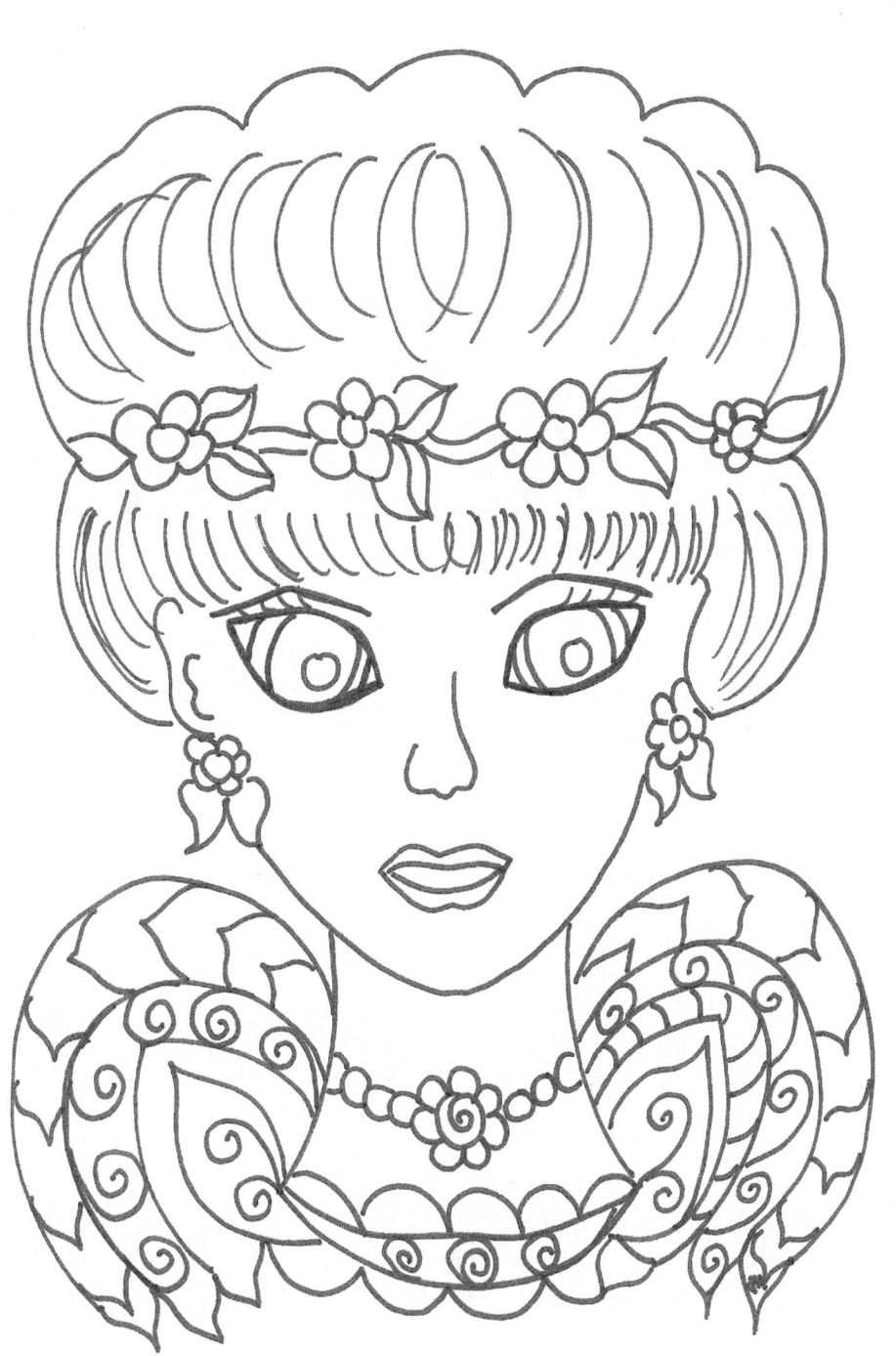

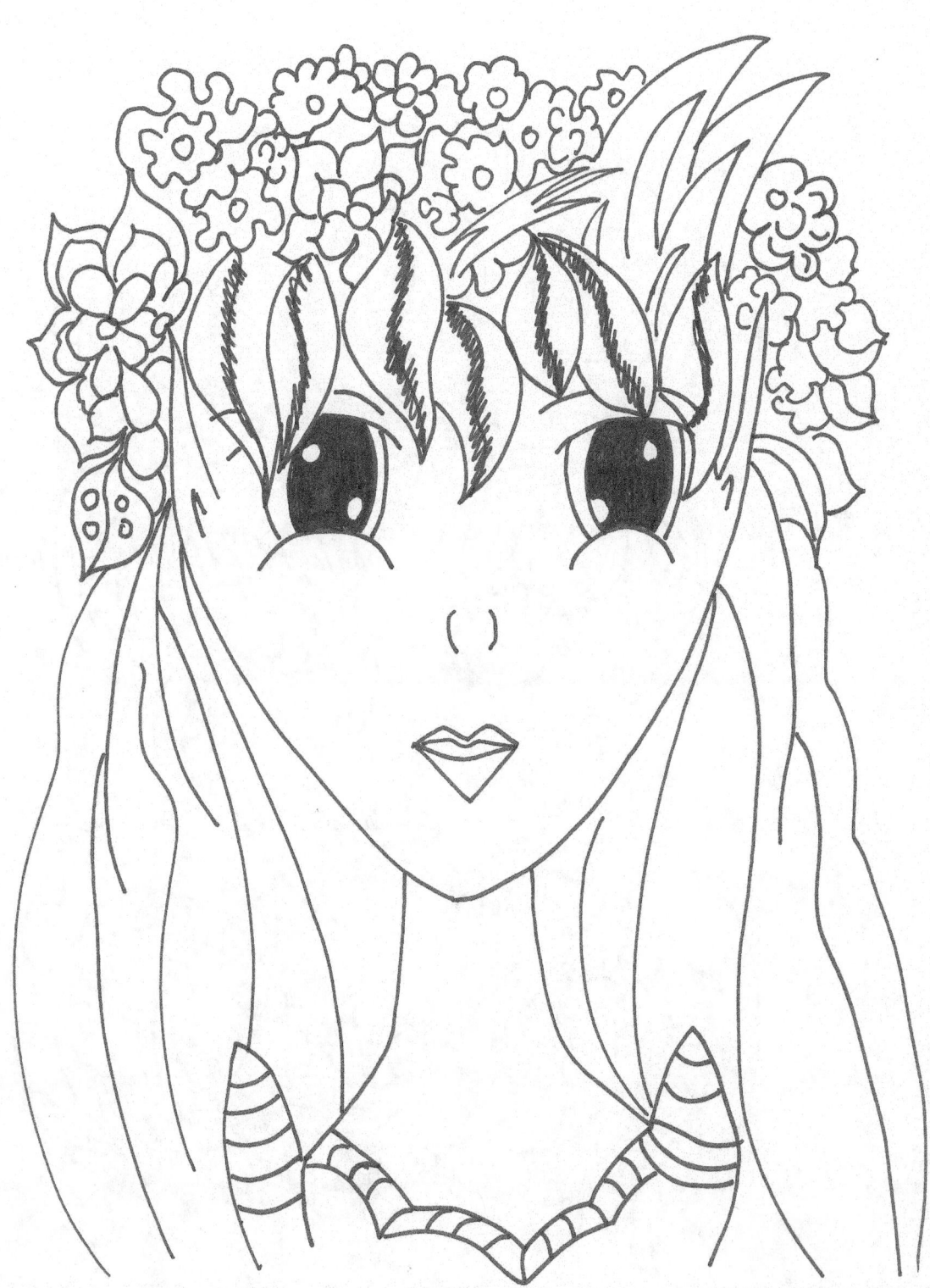

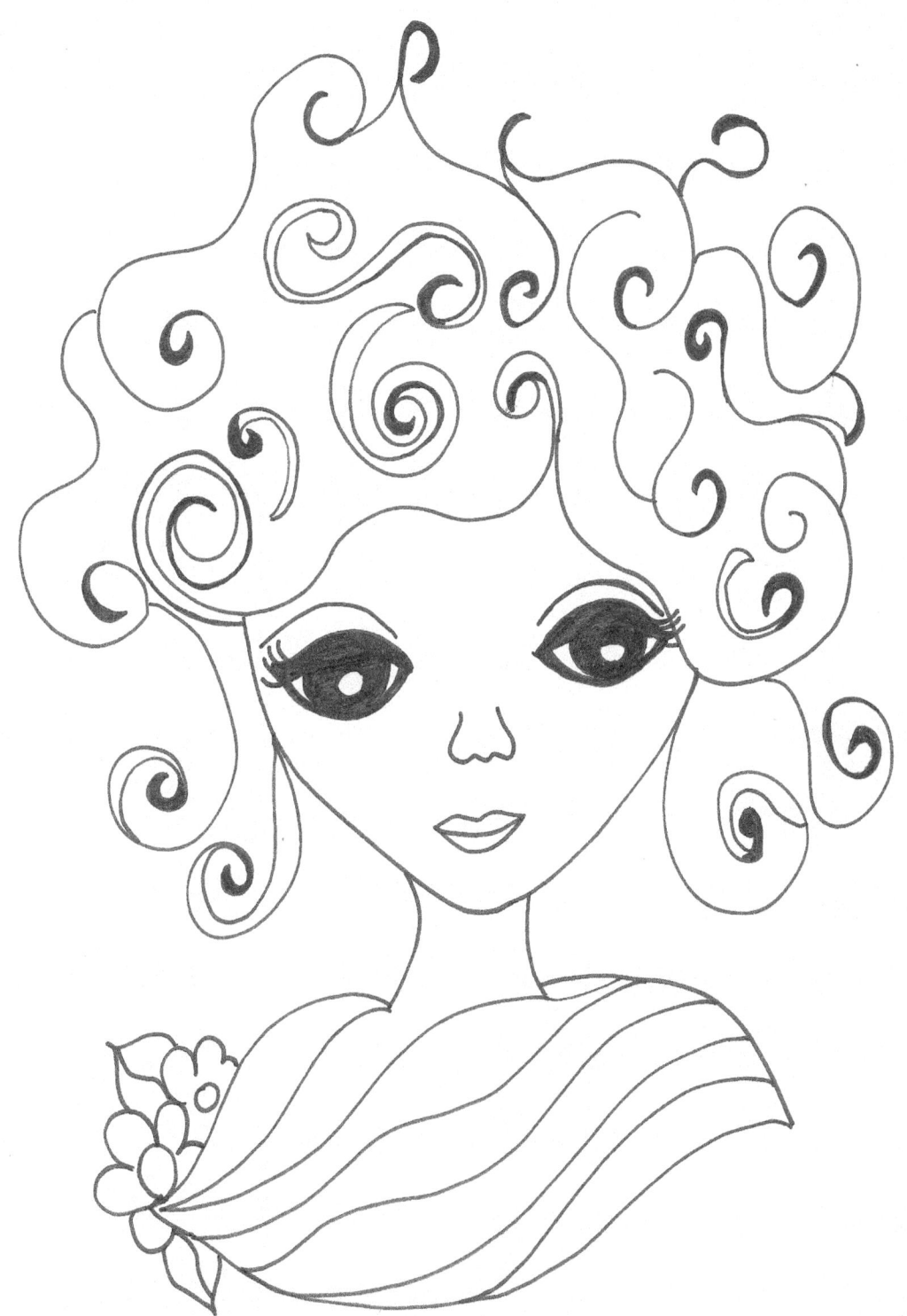

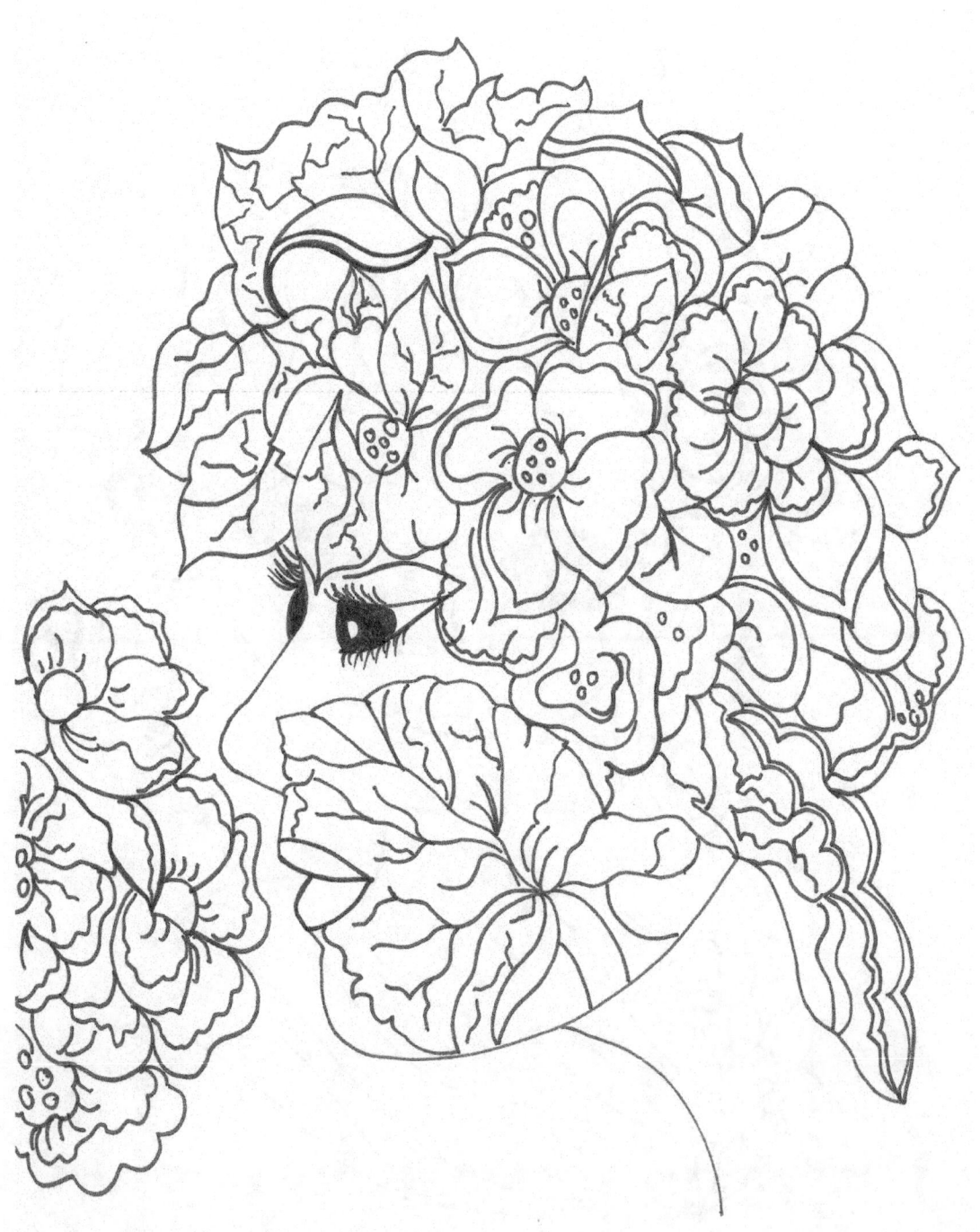

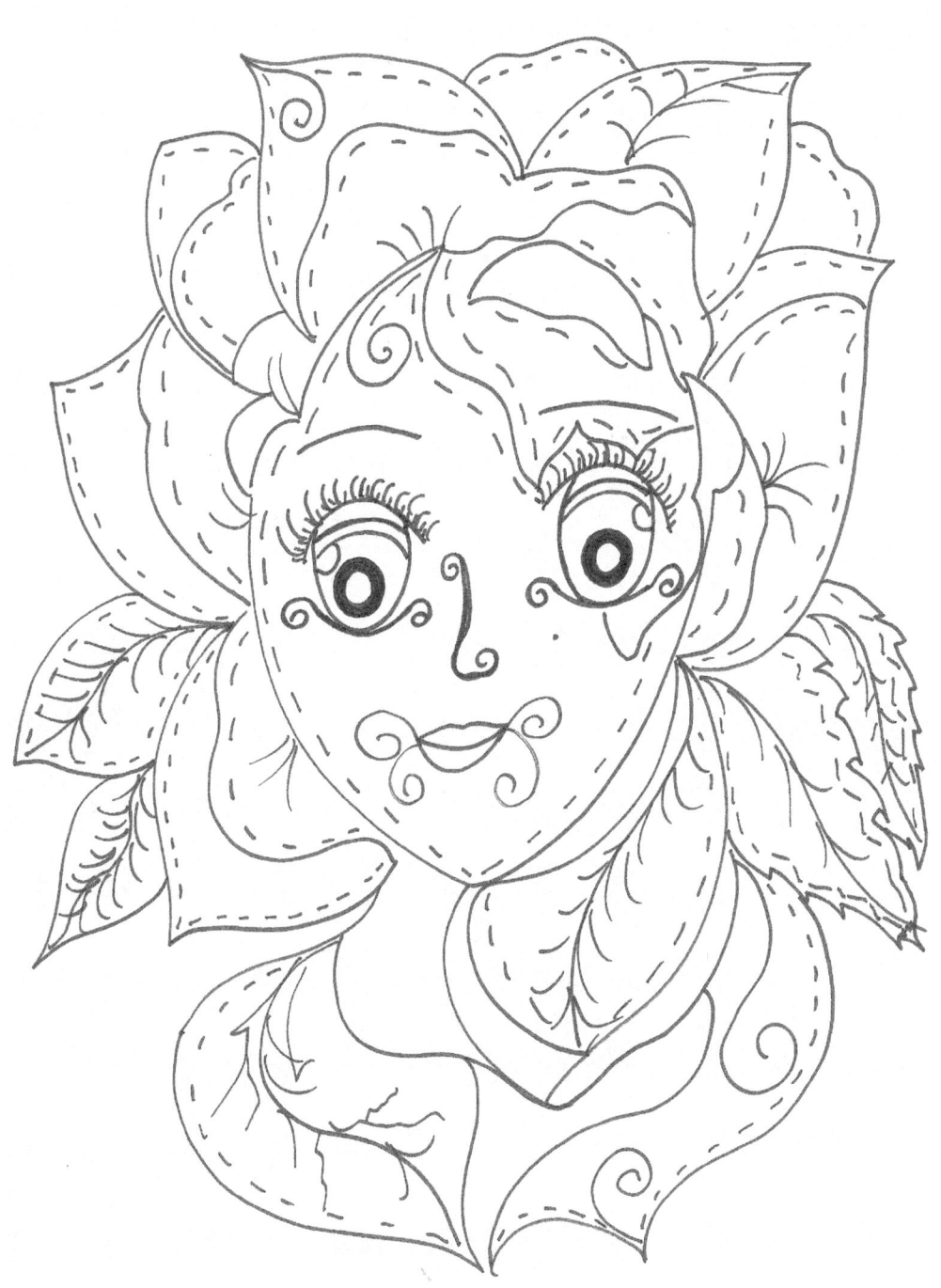

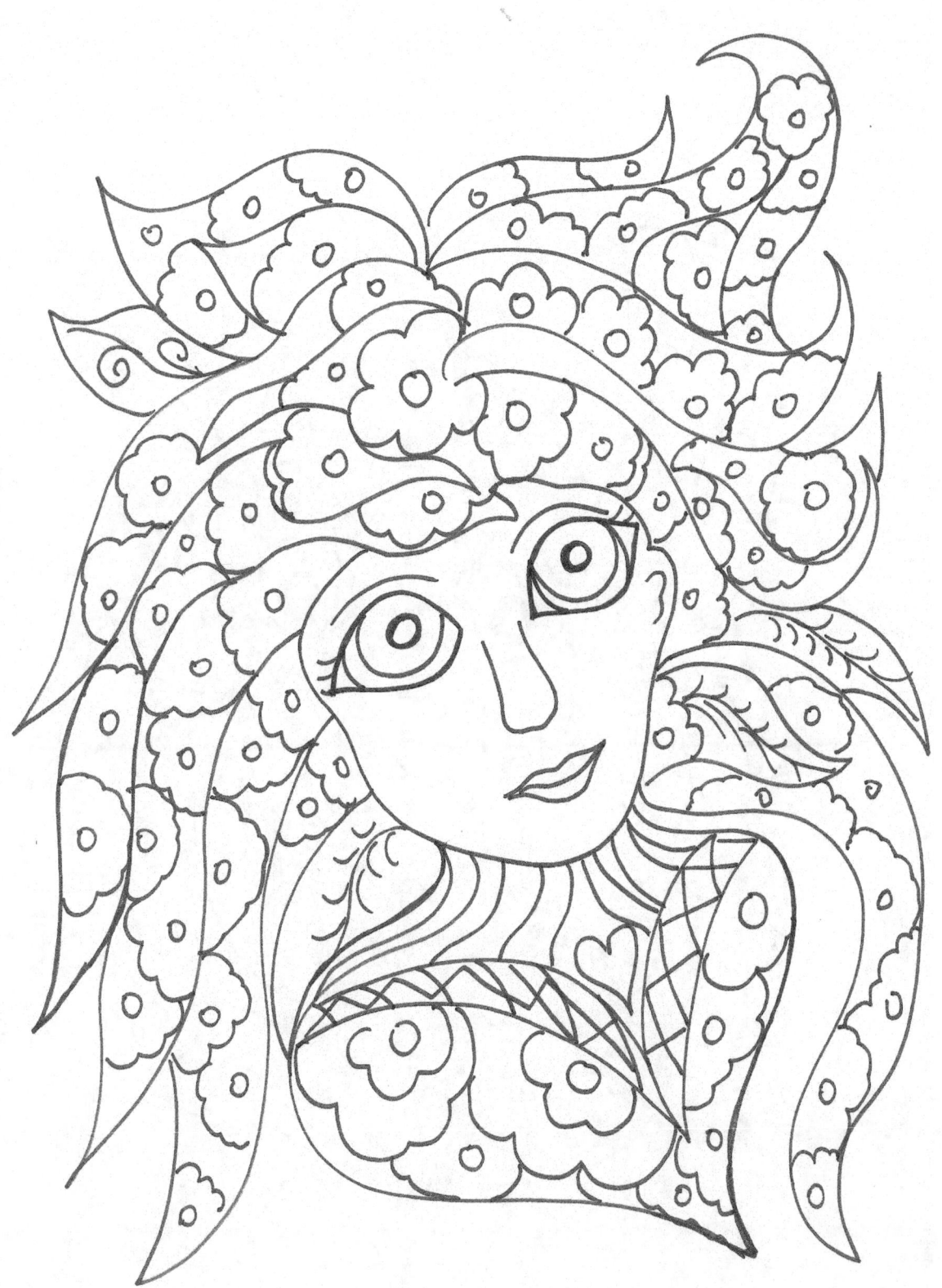

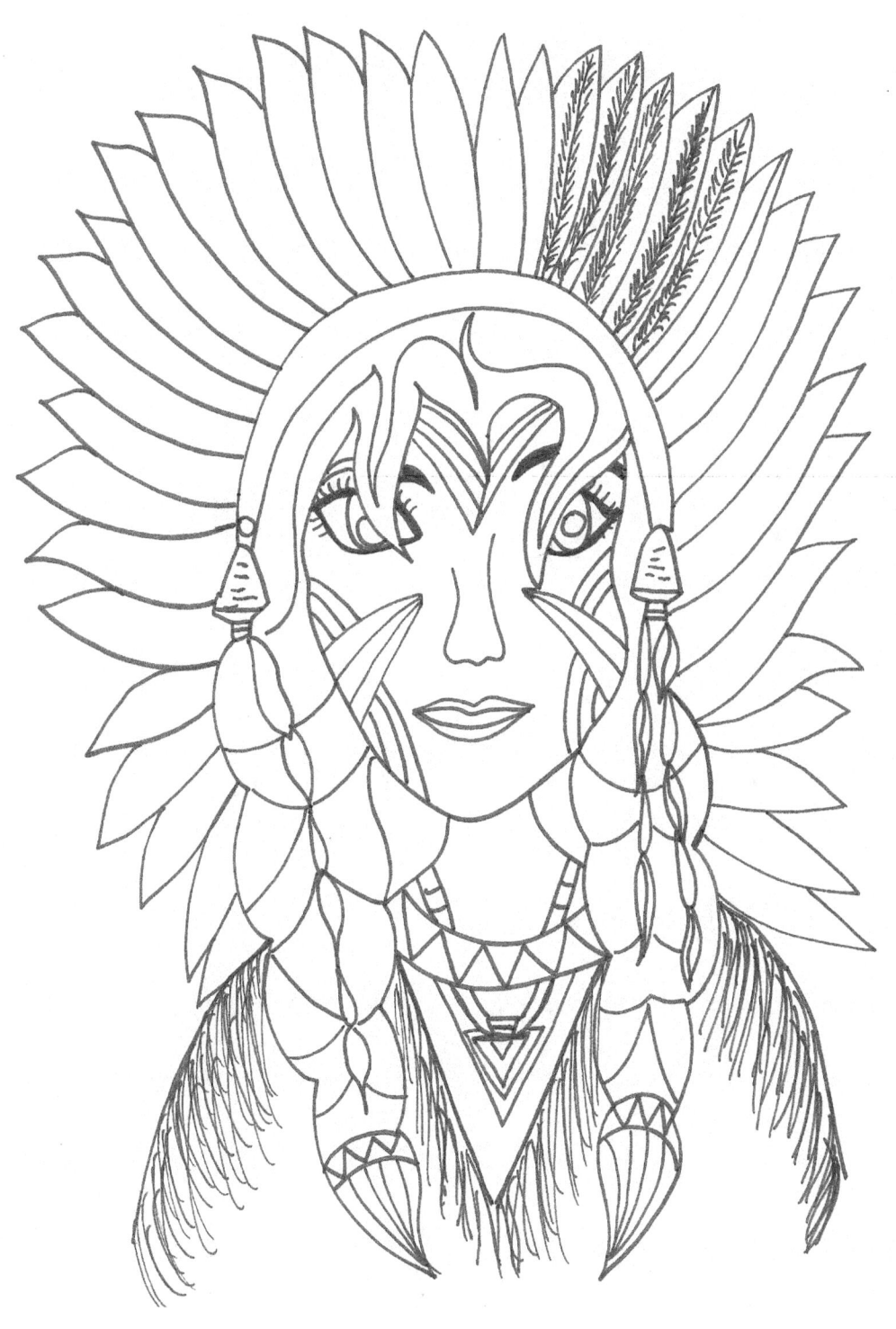

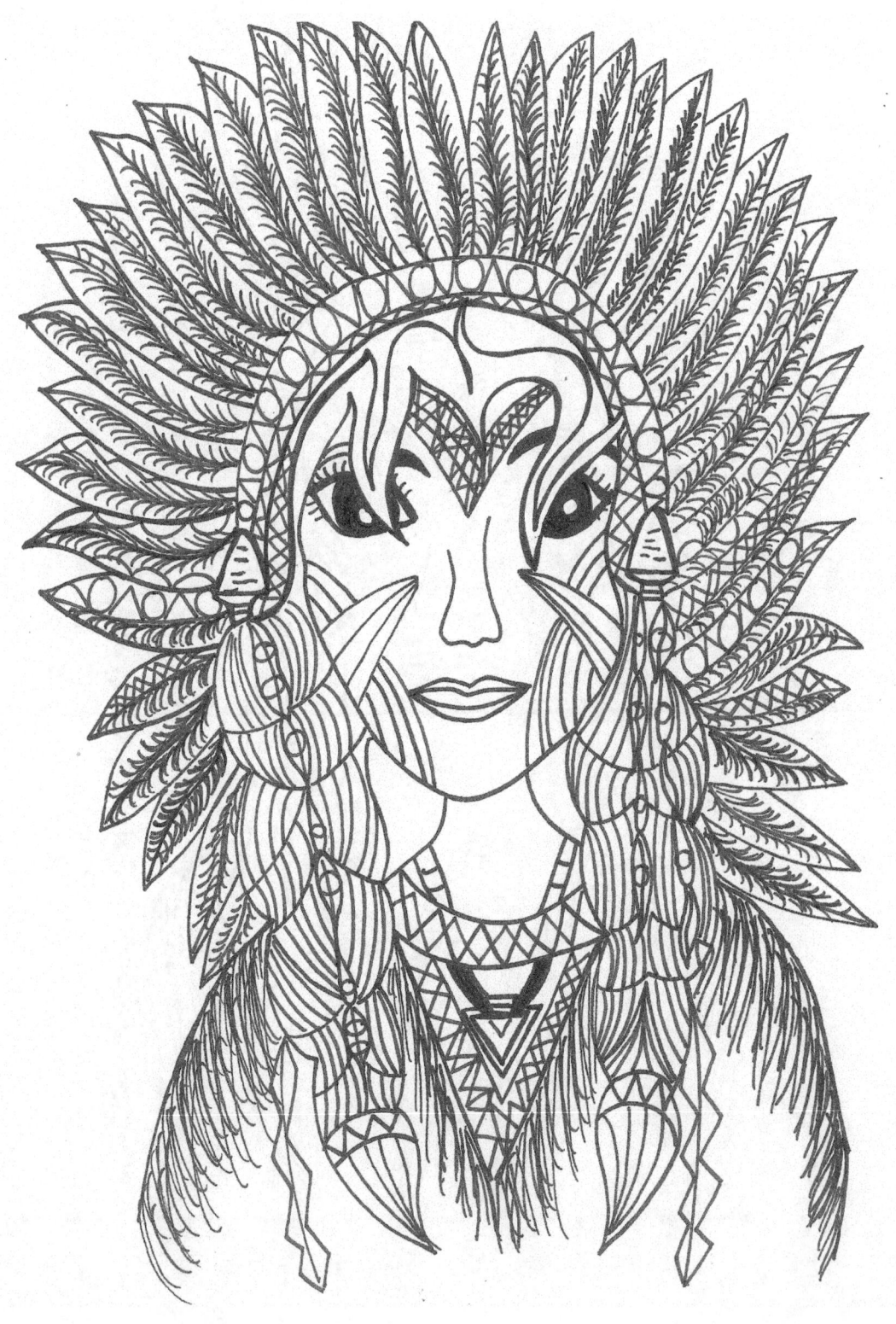

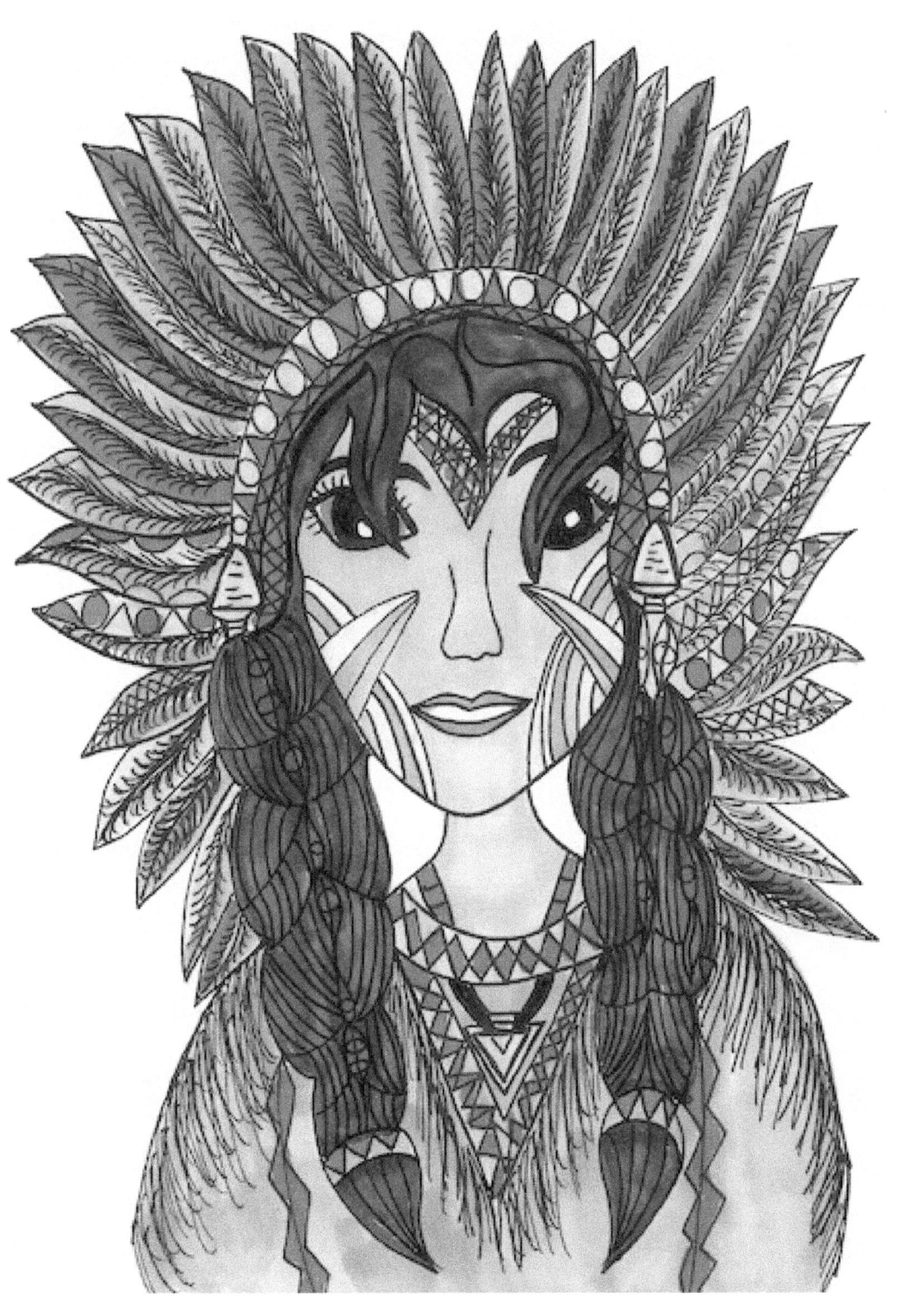

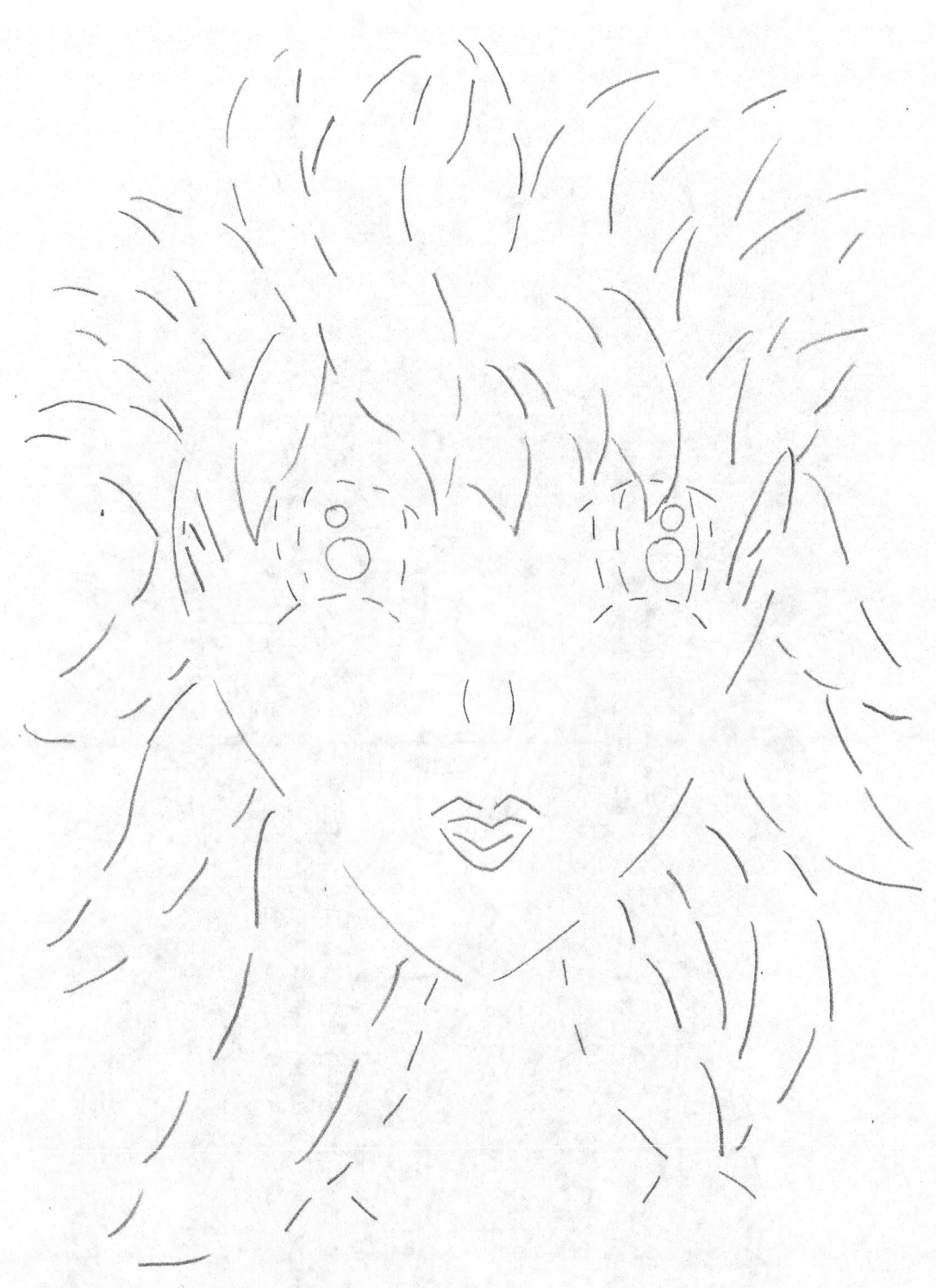

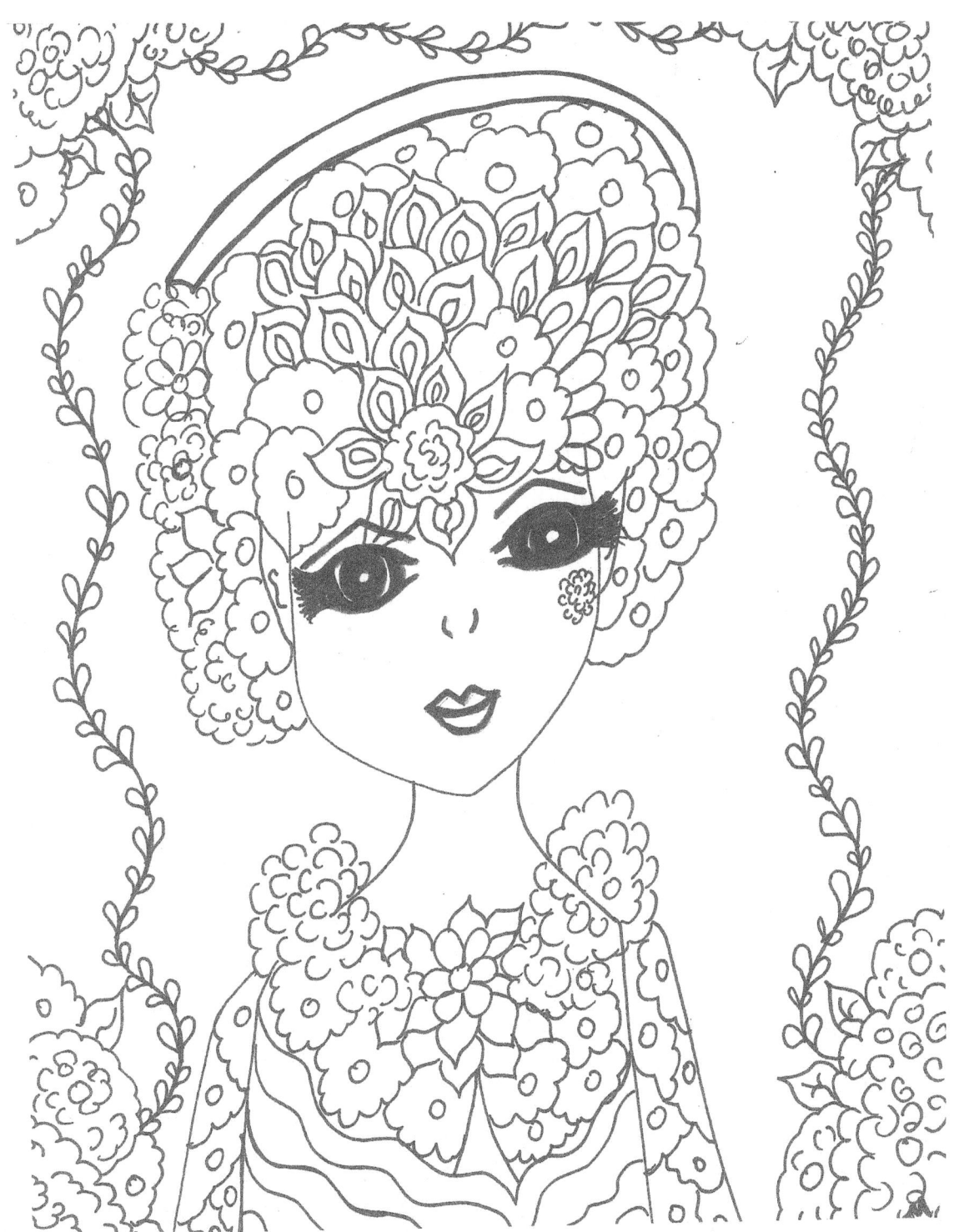

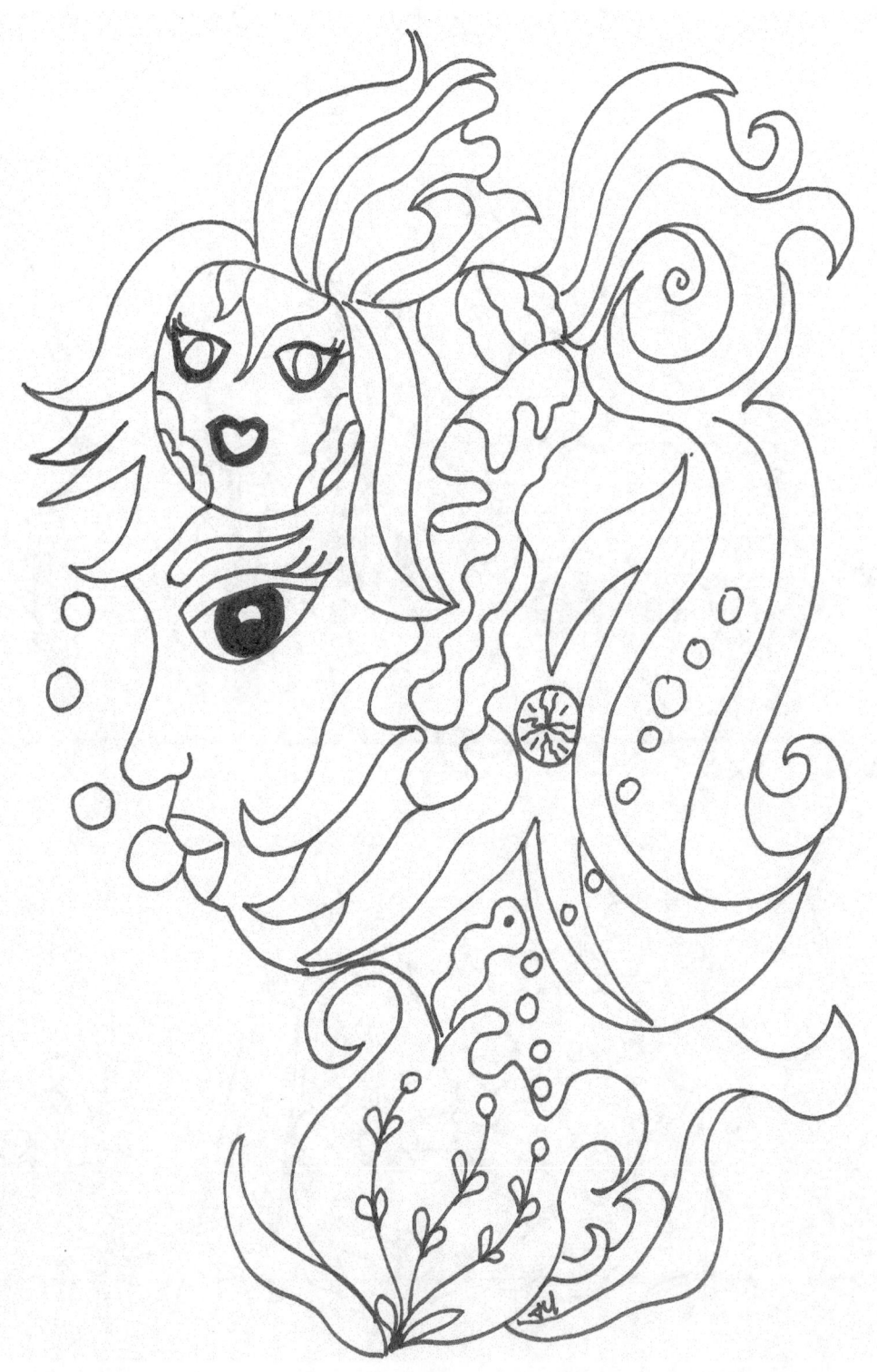

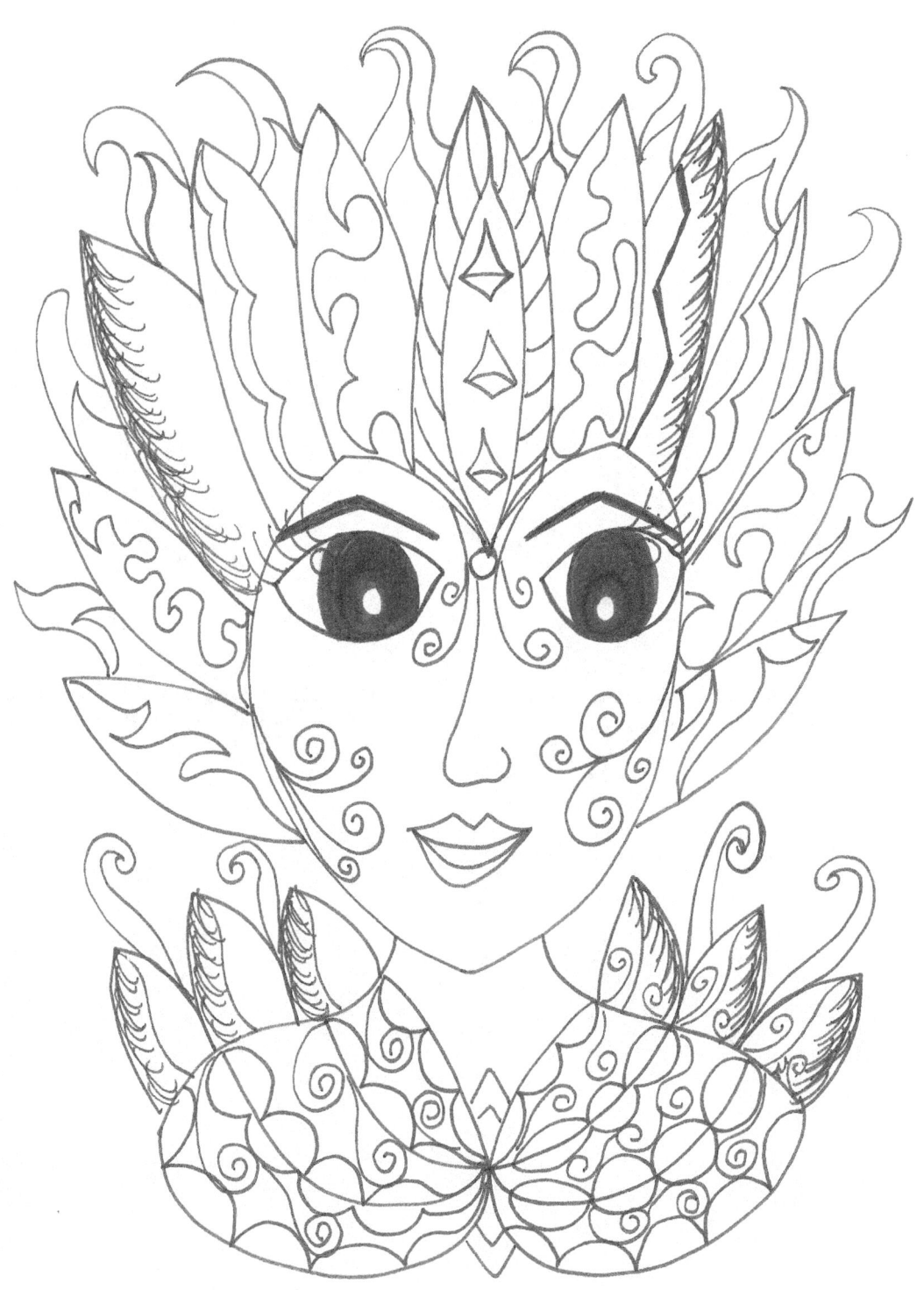

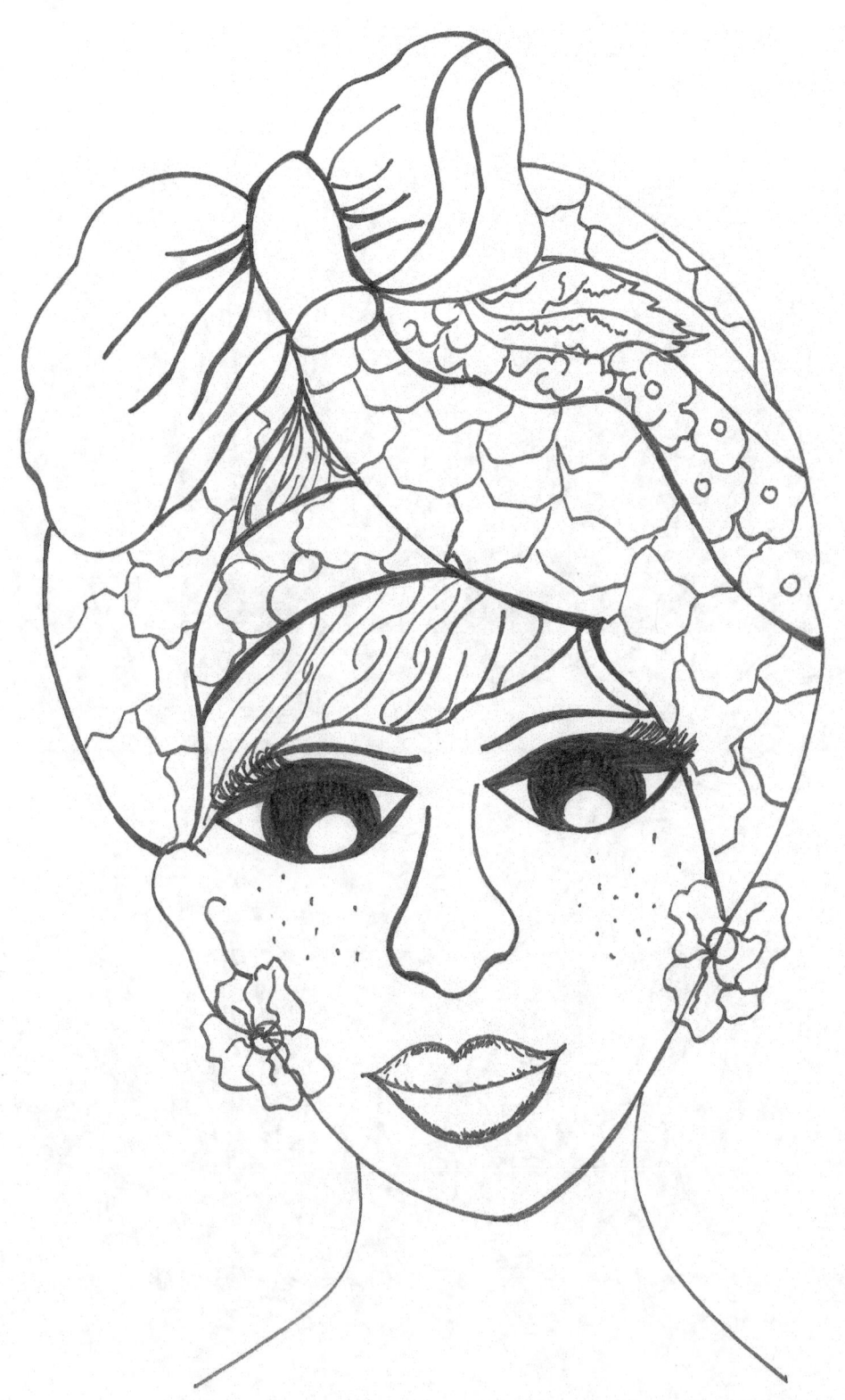

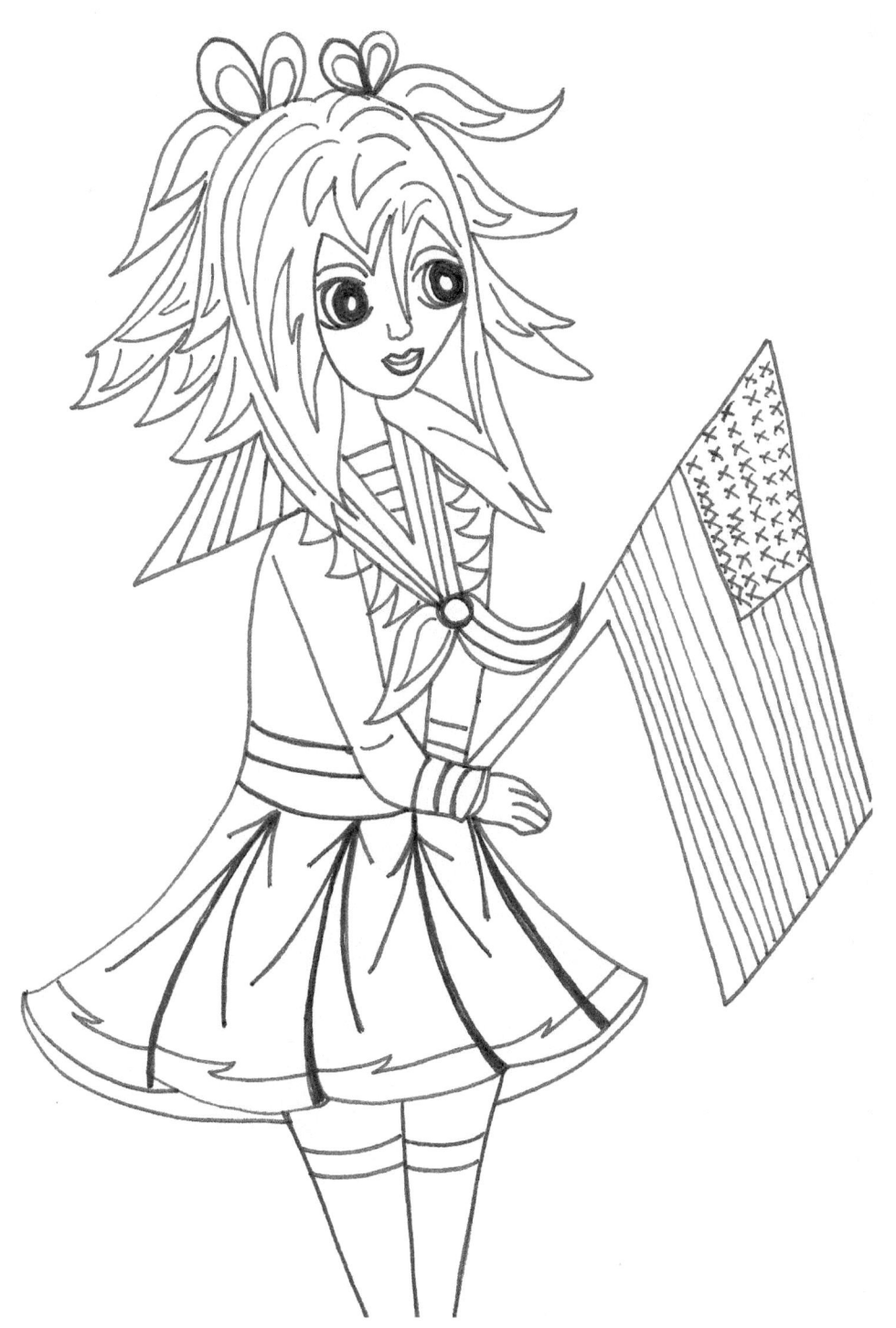

www.ingramcontent.com/pod-product-compliance
Lightning Source LLC
Chambersburg PA
CBHW080624180526
45168CB00007B/3052